W9-ATJ-105

"This above all:
to thine ol' buddy be true."

—*Shakespeare*

A BEST FRIENDS' GUIDE TO LIFE

THE IMPORTANCE OF BEING ERNIE

(and Bert)

SESAME STREET

[Imprint]
MAKE YOUR MARK
NEW YORK

SESAME STREET

[Imprint]
MAKE YOUR MARK

A part of Macmillan Publishing Group, LLC
120 Broadway, New York, NY 10271

Library of Congress Cataloging-in-Publication Data is available.

ISBN 978-1-250-30456-8 (hardcover)

Our books may be purchased in bulk for promotional, educational, or business use. Please
contact your local bookseller or the Macmillan Corporate and Premium Sales Department
at (800) 221-7945 ext. 5442 or by email at MacmillanSpecialMarkets@macmillan.com.

Special thanks to Julie Kraut, a really swell buddy

Book design by Ellen Duda

Imprint logo designed by Amanda Spielman

First edition, 2019

1 3 5 7 9 10 8 6 4 2

In this whole wide world, many types there be;
But all of them must surely agree
This book has a price—it isn't free!
A thief earns no friends. Not even a duckie.

To every Ernie and every Bert out there
(and every Rubber Duckie, too).

1

HOW TO BE
BEST FRIENDS FOREVER

FRIENDSHIP ISN'T A BIG THING.

IT'S A MILLION LITTLE THINGS.

Usually spilled all over the floor.

FINISH *the* SENTENCE

Alone time is . . .

A precious commodity.

Time to wake up Bert.

LIFE IS SHORT.

Spend it with people who let you
try out new knock-knock jokes.

A friend knows the song in your heart and
sings it back to you when you forget the words.

I think the song in my heart
is instrumental.

Good friends will tell you about that
smudge on your face.

TIPS *for* GETTING ALONG

Friends don't keep secrets.

Except for Bert's surprise party next week.

. . . Oops.

Well, Ernie, at least now you're
back to having no secrets.

A friend is someone who knows
everything about you and *still* likes you.

Even after that chocolate
cream pie incident.

A friend always
remembers your birthday.

A *best* friend also
remembers your half-birthday.

I know we're best friends because best friends
bring out the best in each other.

To be clear,
this is your best?

TIPS *for* GETTING ALONG

"A true friend laughs at your jokes,
even when they're not funny."

"HA HA HA!!"

"That wasn't a joke!"

"I'm practicing."

A GOOD FRIEND IS LIKE HOT CHOCOLATE.

Both make you warm and fuzzy inside.

(But hot chocolate never
borrows your socks without asking.)

True friends can comfortably
sit in silence together.

ZEN
SOUND
THE ART O
SILENCE

BUT WHY WOULD THEY?!

TIPS *for* GETTING ALONG

"Bert needs help making new friends,
so sometimes I start conversations with the
person on the other side of him and then stop
talking so they can get to know each other."

"Wait, you've been doing that
ON PURPOSE?"

RUBBER DUCKIE,
YOU'RE THE ONE!

What does
that make me?

A FRIEND IS SOMEONE
WHO LETS YOU BE YOURSELF.

But sometimes wishes you could
be yourself more quietly.

Bert, I think this is the beginning
of a beautiful friendship.

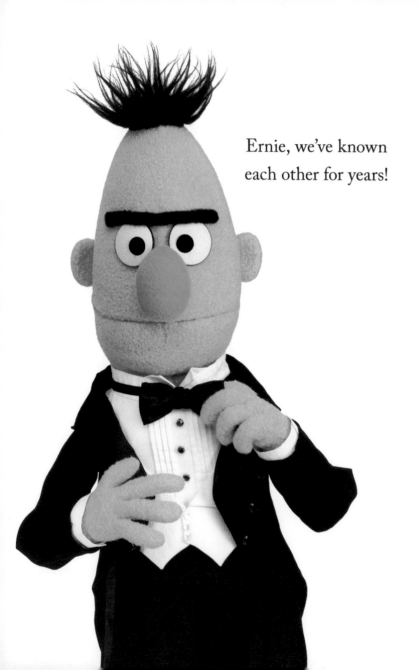

Ernie, we've known
each other for years!

HOW TO BE A
GOOD ROOMMATE

TOP TIPS *for* ROOMMATE LIVING

TREAT OTHERS HOW YOU WANT TO BE TREATED.

Please treat me as described in
the roommate contract you signed.

BEING ROOMMATES MEANS...

ALWAYS HAVING TO SAY YOU'RE SORRY.

TOP TIPS *for* ROOMMATE LIVING

HAVING HOBBIES IS IMPORTANT.

My hobby is doing chores!

"Ernie, Rubber Duckie doesn't pay rent.
That's why he doesn't get a vote."

BERT'S TO-DO LIST

- Clean
- File paperwork
- Create calendar reminders for my coupon expiration dates.
- Make tomorrow's to-do list

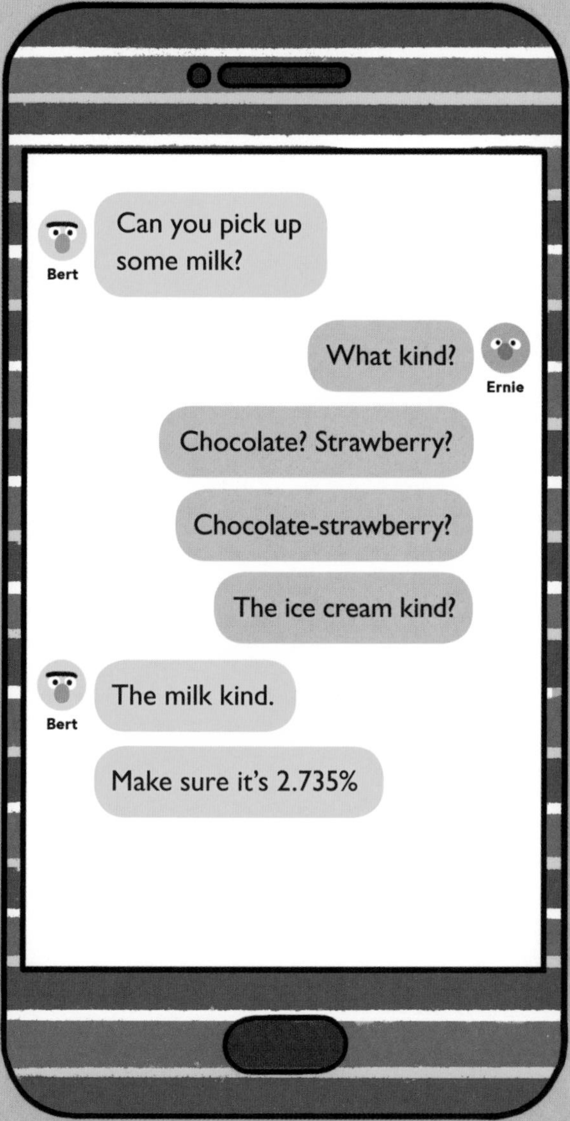
Bert
Can you pick up some milk?
Ernie
What kind?
Chocolate? Strawberry?
Chocolate-strawberry?
The ice cream kind?
Bert
The milk kind.
Make sure it’s 2.735%

TOP TIPS *for* ROOMMATE LIVING

COMMUNICATION
IS KEY.

Say EVERYTHING you're thinking.

TOP TIPS *for* ROOMMATE LIVING

COMMUNICATION IS KEY.

Leave lots of detailed notes.

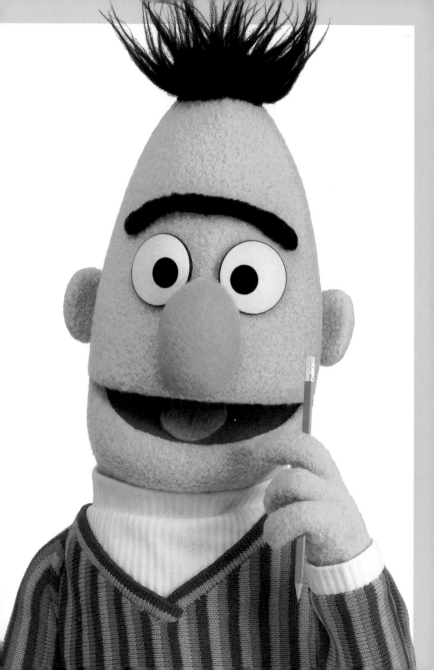

Can I trade my cleanup time

for me time?

Cleanup time *is* me time!

ERNIE

Hey, Bert. I just realized,
today is tomorrow's yesterday . . .
and yesterday, today was tomorrow!

BERT

It's still trash day.
And it's still your turn.

TOP TIPS *for* ROOMMATE LIVING

ALWAYS
BE
YOURSELF.

Sing like nobody's listening . . .
even when your roommate's home.

WHEN ONE DOOR CLOSES—

take it as a signal that quiet time's started.

"Bert, it's not a party! It's just some music, snacks, and forty of our closest friends!"

TOP TIPS *for* ROOMMATE LIVING

HAVE AN EMERGENCY PLAN.

Emergency step one:
find your Rubber Duckie!

Fancy seeing you here!

I live here.

IN THE EYE OF
THE BEHOLDER

WHAT BERT SEES

A rhinoceros.

WHAT ERNIE SEES

A UNICORN!

WHAT BERT SEES

Great for protein.

WHAT ERNIE SEES

Great for juggling.

WHAT ERNIE SEES

Slow down?

WHAT BERT SEES

Stahhhhp. Stop. STOP!!!!!!!!

WHAT BERT SEES

A traffic cone.

WHAT ERNIE SEES

A party hat!

WHAT BERT SEES

An environmental disaster.

WHAT ERNIE SEES

DRUMSTICKS!

WHAT BERT SEES

A tomato.

WHAT ERNIE SEES

Future pizza!

WHAT BERT SEES

A huge mess. Absolutely no glitter in the
apartment, ever. We've discussed this.

WHAT ERNIE SEES

MAGIC

WHAT BERT SEES

One of my favorite things!

WHAT ERNIE SEES

What is that?

WHAT ERNIE SEES

Ice cream sundae toppers!

WHAT BERT SEES

An indelible stain waiting to happen.

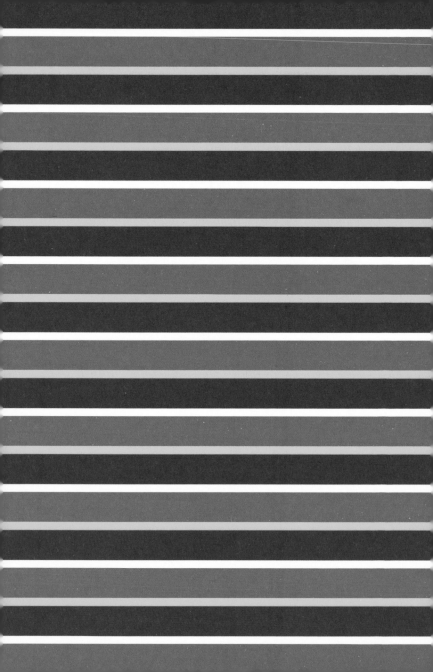

WORDS TO LIVE BY

SEIZE THE MOMENT!

After you check your
day planner and confirm
you're available!

FINISH *the* SENTENCE

A journey of a thousand steps begins with . . .

Lots of stretching, then planning your route with bathroom stops and all necessary supplies.

Oooh, that sounds like a lot of steps!
I want to try it!
Let's see: one, two, three, four, five, six, seven, eight, nine, ten, eleven, twelve, thirteen . . .

You can't be late if you don't
set a time in the first place.

It's not whether you win or lose,
it's how you play the game.

Wait, we didn't
agree on the
rules yet!

PARTY GAMES
and How to
Avoid Them

THE BEST THINGS IN LIFE ARE FREE!

But I bring coupons just in case.

ALWAYS WALK ON THE SUNNY SIDE OF THE STREET.

And don't forget to wear sunscreen.

You know, Ernie, I always say:
Actions speak louder than words.

Except when the word is

ACTION!

LOCATION:

SESAME ST.

DIRECTOR:

B. BIRD

GROWING UP ISN'T EASY.

So why do it?

ENJOY NATURE'S SPLENDOR!

IT'S ALWAYS
SWEATER WEATHER
SOMEWHERE!

LAUGHTER MAKES THE WORLD GO ROUND.

Huh, I'm pretty sure the earth
spins due to angular momentum . . .

FINISH *the* SENTENCE

You live, you learn . . .

And then what happens?

True, but you're missing a few middle steps.
To learn correctly you need index cards, highlighter
pens, notebooks, an online study forum, and—
if you have a certain roommate—a very
powerful white-noise machine.

EYES ARE THE WINDOW TO THE SOUL.

And eyebrows are super important, too.

ARE YOU A BERT
or AN ERNIE?

WHAT IS THE BEST THING TO PUT ON TOAST?

A. Nothing. Dry toast? It's the perfect food.

B. Everything! Anything!

FOR EXERCISE, I LIKE TO . . .

A. Meditate.

B. Jazzercise!

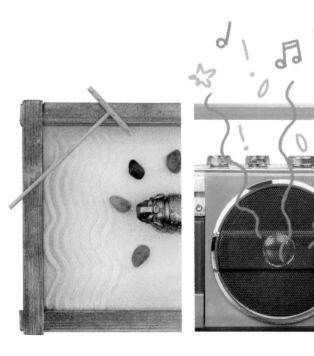

COMPLETE THIS SENTENCE: TURTLENECKS ARE GREAT FOR . . .

A. Warmth.

B. Layering, pretending to be Bert, pretending to be a turtle, sticking your head under the neck part and pretending your head is missing...

DO YOU USUALLY KNOW WHAT TIME IT IS?

A. Of course.

B. Party time!

WHAT'S YOUR FAVORITE SUBJECT IN SCHOOL?

A. Grammar.

B. Recess.

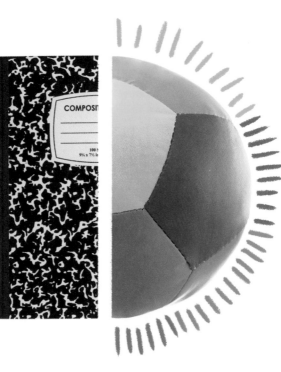

WHEN YOU WAKE UP IN THE MORNING, WHAT GETS YOU GOING?

A. Making my bed. Hospital corners are my jam.

B. A big breakfast and three-hour drum session.

ARE YOU A PEOPLE PERSON?

A. No.

B. I'm a people, dogs, birds, rubber duckies, and confetti person! I guess I'm kind of an everything person.

WHAT'S THE BEST THING ABOUT NATURE?

A. Sunsets.

B. Mud.

WHAT'S YOUR FAVORITE COLOR?

A. Beige.

B. Rainbow.

WHERE IS YOUR HAPPY PLACE?

A. Anywhere there's something for me to clean or organize.

B. Anywhere I can dance.

ARE YOU AN EARLY BIRD OR A NIGHT OWL?

A. Early bird.

B. I'm more of a rubber duckie.

WHERE'S YOUR FAVORITE PLACE IN THE WORLD?

A. Anywhere quiet.

B. Anywhere with Bert—and hopefully also a musical instrument.

DO YOU DO TASKS RIGHT AWAY OR DO YOU PROCRASTINATE?

A. Right away.

B. Right away! Although maybe not the tasks I'm tasked with. But I'm doing tasks!

WHAT'S ONE THING YOU'LL NEVER GET TIRED OF?

A. Alphabetizing.

B. Breakfast for dinner. In footie pajamas!

WHO ARE YOU?

If you chose mostly A answers:

You are a Bert. Completing this quiz might have been very satisfying for you, as quizzes and tests often are. You may even have taken careful notes. And filed them.

If you chose mostly B answers:

You are an Ernie. You may have found it difficult to pay strict attention at every moment to this quiz—and possibly to this very sentence. You may even have already left the room.

FAMOUS BERTS
AND ERNIES

Albert Einstein

Once Ernie's Theory of Rubber Duckativity
is proven, this will make more sense.

Charles Darwin

They both have evolved sensibilities.

Mother Teresa

You'd understand why if you ever saw her play drums.
Oh, and . . . unconditional love!

Steve Jobs

They share an affinity for black turtlenecks.

Vincent van Gogh

Like van Gogh, Ernie sees a few more colors
than most of us.

Abraham Lincoln

Like Abe, Bert is very honest—especially when it comes to who has and has not done their chores.

Sigmund Freud

Both want to hear all about your dreams—
and believe that sometimes a banana is just
a banana. And sometimes a telephone.

Queen Victoria

Both are well-known for their strong support
of the British Reform Act of 1867.

CELEBRATE
YOUR DIFFERENCES

FINISH *the* SENTENCE

I never make the same mistake twice, because . . .

I journal about all my mistakes for
twenty minutes before bed each night.

Why settle for only twice?

WHAT WE'RE READING

ONE HUNDRED YEARS OF SOLITUDE AND OTHER DREAM VACATION IDEAS

PET PEEVES OF HIGHLY EFFECTIVE PEOPLE

The Life-Changing Magic of Tidying Up... After Someone Else

THE FAULT IN OUR ROOMMATES

HOW TO WIN FRIENDS and Alienate Roommates

The Curious Incident of the Cookies I Ate in Bed in the Nighttime

GONE WITH THE WIND and Other Possible Explanations for What Happened to My Passport

Wake me when it's
BATH TIME.

I don't know why I check the time.
I know I'm early.

Wish List

- New shoe insoles.
- Government bonds for Bernice, my pigeon. She needs a nice nest egg.
- Computer paper. Ooh, dot matrix!
- File folders. ~~Manila.~~ No! Go wild: <u>Mauve!</u>
- Khakis.

I celebrate my

BIRTHDAY,
HALF-BIRTHDAY,
QUARTER-BIRTHDAY,
EIGHTH-BIRTHDAY,
AND SIXTEENTH-BIRTHDAY.

It's a lot of work,
but I'm worth it!

Work is hard, Ernie.

So is a rock!
And juggling!

WHAT?

Oh, weren't we listing
stuff that's hard?

FINISH *the* SENTENCE

There is no such thing as too many . . .

Bouncy houses!

Paper clips!

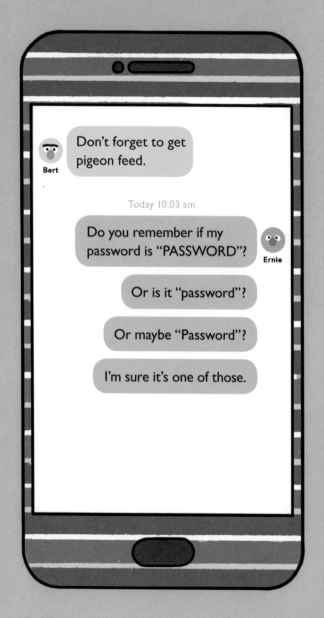

Ernie, if you ever walked
a mile in my shoes—

I ALREADY DID!

Is that how they got all
muddy and scuffed?

!?!

OVERHEARD *on* SESAME STREET

Where are all our shoes?

I traded them in for roller skates.

We live in a walk-up.

I know! See you downstairs!

"Aren't airports great, Bert? Everybody's going somewhere new, something exciting is always happening, and it's perfect for people-watching."

"Ernie, airports are crowded and everyone's angry and worrying they didn't pack enough socks and racing to get to the plane in time. No one loves airports."

"But Bert, Oscar the Grouch loves airports!"

"Exactly."

ERNIE'S TO-DO LIST

BERT'S TO-DO LIST

- Reorganize grocery store's soda section by bottle cap color. (They'll thank me once they see the end result.)
- Clean out dryer lint

  ☆ Sort paper clips

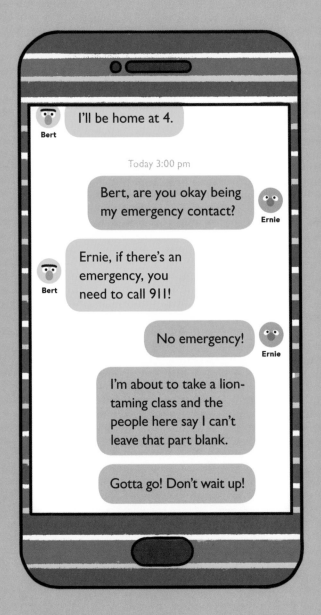

ACKNOWLEDGMENTS

BERT: I would like to thank my best friend, Ernie, and my pigeon, Bernice.

ERNIE: I would like to thank my best friend, Bert, and my Rubber Duckie and everyone on Sesame Street, especially Big Bird and Snuffy and Oscar the Grouch and Slimey and Cookie Monster and Zoe and Rocco and Rosita and Grover and the Count and Prairie Dawn and Elmo and Abby Cadabby and Rudy and Julia and Telly and Murray and Gordon and Susan and Miles and Mr. Hooper and Mr. Handford and Willy and Miguel and Rafael and Ruthie and Buffy and Olivia and Jason and Bob and Linda and Luis and Maria and Gabi and Lillian and Leela and Jelani and Gina and Tarah and David and Chris and Celina and Carlo and Alan and Nina and Mr. Noodle . . .

ABOUT THE AUTHORS

Ernie is a fan of staying up late, taking baths with Rubber Duckie, and playing the saxophone. He lives with his ol' buddy Bert on Sesame Street.

Bert enjoys reading, collecting paper clips, and eating food that is very bland. He lives with his best friend, Ernie, on Sesame Street.

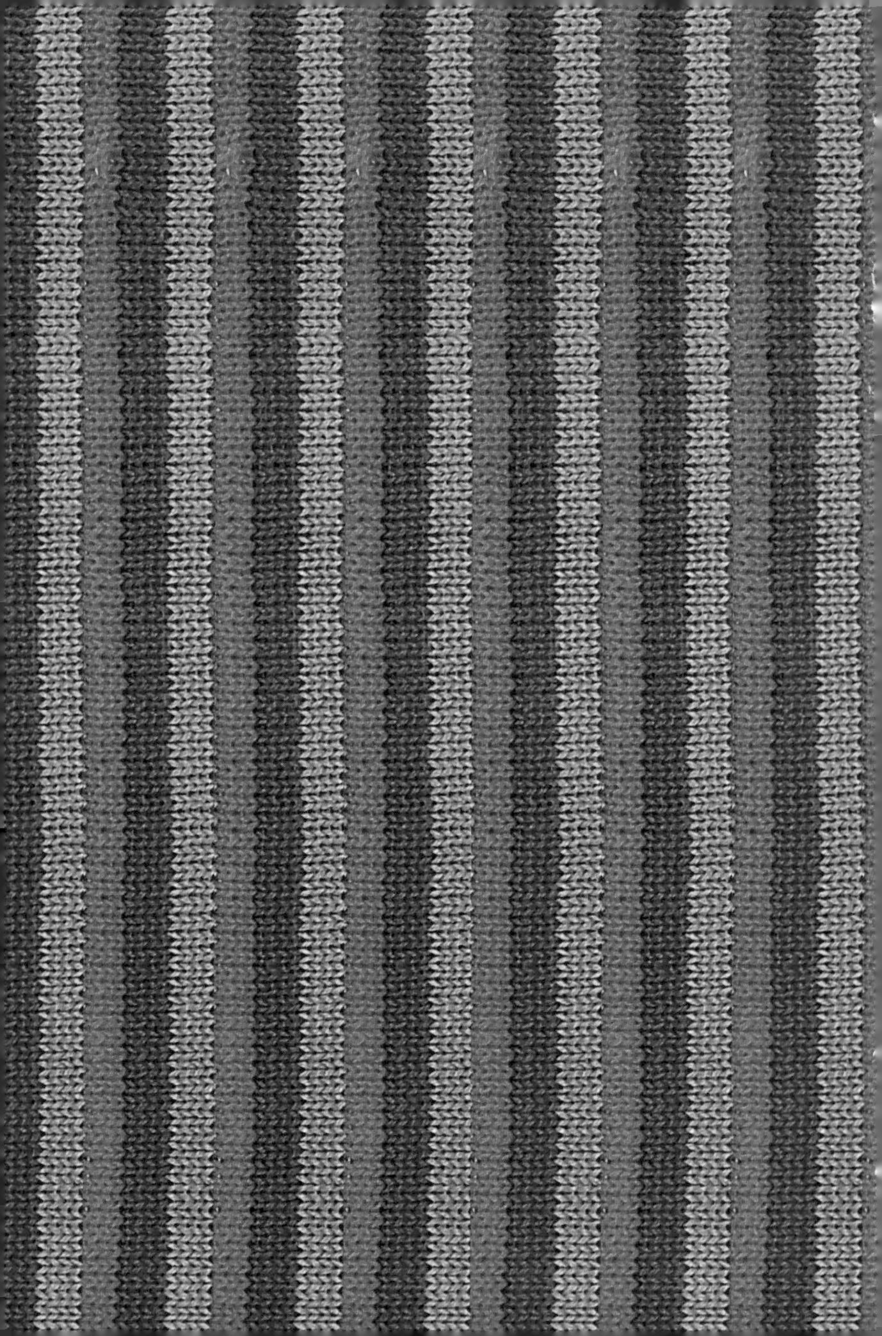